Simply Content

Finding Freedom in a Culture of Excess

Valorie Bender Quesenberry

wesleyan
publishing
house

Indianapolis, Indiana

To the Reader

I write to you as a friend—as a fellow journeyer on the trek toward knowing God in new and intimate ways. Like you, I have a longing to know who He is, what He wants from me, and what He has planned for me. So I've been getting to know the many women whose stories appear in His Word, and I have come to understand many new truths about the real purpose God had when He created woman.

I invite you on this journey of discovery. We'll meet women from varied circumstances who found God faithful and true to His Word; sisters in faith who faced the same struggles we face.

This is a journey that has a great deal of relevance to our lives today. You'll also read brief snippets from women of our time who are demonstrating what it means to put Bible lessons into practice.

You may choose to take this journey alone or as part of a small group or Bible class. If you take it alone, I challenge you to find a trusted friend who can help you process the decisions you'll make along the way. If you choose to take this journey as part of a group meeting, take some time before your meeting to read **For Openers**, **Getting to Know Her**, and the Scripture passage for that week.

So, come on. Let me introduce you to some amazing sisters and women who touched the heart of God.

To the Leader

I hope you're excited about this journey. The women of the Bible have so much to teach women today. As a leader, you'll have the privilege of shepherding group members in their discussions and commitments. It is important that you personally prepare for each session by reading the text and praying for God's guidance and leadership.

The first two sections of each week's session—**For Openers** and **Getting to Know Her**—should take about one-fourth of your total session time. Reading and discussing the next two sections— **The Word Speaks** and **Where We Come In**—along with the sidebars will make up the majority of your session. Try to leave about a quarter of your session time on the response sections— **Responding through Prayer**, **My Next Step**, and **Keep It in Mind**.

After the first week, begin each session by asking participants how they applied the previous week's commitments. Encourage the group members to share freely about their successes and struggles and to support one another. Do this shepherding prayerfully and with the grace and compassion that can flow only from a relationship with Jesus Christ.

May God's presence be felt in your group and its members come to know Him in new and fresh ways.

Contents

Acknowledgements

N o person's writings have shaped my thinking on surrendered living more than those of Elisabeth Elliot. In her words, I have encountered the cross at every turn. The many quotes in this manuscript reflect the value and validity of her insight. I recommend her books to all who would learn the joy of Calvary living.

This study of contentment has challenged and convicted me. Along the way, I have been gifted with support from family and friends whose willingness to discuss this topic has been invaluable in the thinking and writing process. I must in particular express my appreciation to:

My friends in Christ—your desire to know Him better pulls me along with you; I'm blessed to have so many "sisters."

My parents—it was around our family table that I first learned to delight in the discussion of biblical truth; as your daughter, I am greatly indebted, and I love you always.

Kevin—you believed this idea could grow into a book; thanks for being there for every stage from brainstorming to editing—as usual, the manuscript benefited from your touch.

Jody—it's been inspiring to discuss with you the nuances of important words and the hidden meanings of biblical concepts; your insights have been a gift.

Liz—the authenticity you exhibit in your walk with Christ convicts and encourages me; I'm grateful you shared your journey toward contentment with me.

Becky—every time I see you, there's a new chapter in our journal of faith; I've liked knowing that someone else was experiencing the adventure with me—I wonder what's next . . . ?

Crystal—it's been heartening to share the path toward contentment with a faithful friend like you; thank you for listening to my growing pains along the way and for often reminding me that He is ever working for our good.

Jim—they say siblings are the closest blood relation, but we're also kindred spirits in our love of discovery and debate; you helped me gel my thoughts so many times—thank you.

Danny—God's path for you has involved some difficult turns, but you haven't become bitter; may I accept the twists in my life with similar grace—you inspire me.

Joy—when we were younger, contentment meant hours to play and dream; now that we're grown, it means trusting God with each new season of life—thanks for being there.

Ashley, Autumn, Stewart, and Kaley—being your mom is a task prodigious in its responsibility and incredible in its reward; I will count myself successful if I can stir in your hearts an appetite for the deep riches found in Christ.

Duane—an untold amount of credit is really yours; for believing in my abilities, for encouraging me when I'm overwhelmed, for sharing your scriptural research and interpretation, for taking on kitchen duties when I'm writing, for loving and supporting me—you're quite a guy. I love you more than ever.

Father God—Your ways are so much higher than mine; in the dark days, You didn't leave, and in the desert places, You were faithful. Help me hold fast to the eternal riches that never fade and let me learn to be simply content in You.

Introduction

This was a difficult book to write. Getting a firm grasp on the concept of contentment is not an easy task.

For one thing, the word *content* encompasses many nuances. It is a notion that can apply to almost any facet of life, from bank accounts to body shape. Despite its evasive qualities, contentment is a topic which I believe interests many women, though they may not even realize it. I think that interest is illustrated in the astounding success of the genre of fiction known as Amish novels. The reading public's passion for this line of literature has baffled editors and publishers from the beginning. I believe a large part of the appeal is the allure of a simple life where, except for the difficulties of the romance plot, the characters seem to live happy and peaceful (contented) lives.

Still, contentment is a theme that often induces guilt. This study was particularly poignant for me because of circumstances in my own life that forced me to grapple more personally with this important biblical topic. And as I dug deeper, I was amazed to discover the myriad of ways contentment intersects with other scriptural principles. And I began to realize that this quaint idea is actually relevant for twenty-first-century women after all.

What Is It, Exactly?

Contentment is a slippery concept. Because it is so vital to our Christian growth, I believe Satan has tried to keep us confused about what it really is.

For starters, it isn't happiness. Recently, a friend and I were discussing the fact that the word *happy* comes from two roots, *hap* (chance, fortune) and *y* (glad), giving the impression of a positive feeling resulting from chance events. I haven't found anybody who is content by accident or coincidence; therefore, the definition must go beyond mere happiness.

Nor is it an emotion. In Philippians 4:11, the apostle Paul wrote that he was content—under house arrest, chained to a Roman guard. Certainly, he didn't have warm, fuzzy feelings about that arrangement.

On the other hand, it isn't nonchalance. It seems to us sometimes that the most contented people are those who care little "if school keeps or not" so to speak. But that isn't so. A no-care attitude may simply indicate a lack of comprehension or little sense of responsibility. Those who are truly content care deeply about life and their circumstances; they have developed the trait on purpose.

Then again, it isn't austerity. By nature, some folks prefer a no-nonsense type of life. They are not particularly fond of convenience or luxury. It seems they get their greatest thrills in life from enduring hardship. So, they would likely struggle even to recognize contentment; to them, ease and enjoyment are foreign so they don't expect them.

So, exactly what is this elusive, but essential trait? Contentment is an attitude. It is a deliberate choice. It isn't dependent on feelings, circumstances, or personal temperament. It's a character trait that anyone can develop.

Contentment is freedom. It is personal liberty from greed. In a culture obsessed with always having more, it is a self-declared proclamation of exemption.

Contentment is a statement of value. It's the gold standard of the currency of my life. As long as I possess what is most valuable to me, all else is expendable. This is why the apostle Paul could say that he counted "everything a loss" for the knowledge of Christ (Phil. 3:7–8). His most precious treasure was Christ; in comparison, no other loss could shake his foundation.

By contrast, discontent is an undue focus on self. Self-centeredness is at the core of sin: "It's all about me and what I want." Satan was the first created being to indulge in discontent. He wanted more glory for himself; he coveted God's place. For that, he was cast out of heaven. Now he roams our globe, tempting us to mimic his sin.

Because of the void caused by the entrance of sin into our world, we have within us this unquenchable thing called appetite, an ever-present desire for more. Every person alive has felt its gnawing in the soul. Satan offers to fill the hunger with an ever-present array of earthly indulgences. But we get into trouble when we buy into the philosophy that happiness is either "more than I have" or "different than what I have."

How Do I Become Content?

My brother shared with me his thought that contentment is "the result of a self-determined process." I think that says it pretty well.

In Philippians 4:11, the apostle Paul said that he had *learned* to be content in whatever situation he found himself. That tells me being content is a process God works in us.

Many of us struggle with things that require process. In our microwavable, instant-message-driven culture, we are accustomed to immediate solutions. We feed growth hormones to our chickens so we can get them into the casserole sooner, and we use Miracle-Gro on our vegetable gardens so we can hasten their journey to our tables. In our spiritual lives, we become impatient with the daily discipline of building spiritual muscle. Can't we hurry up and get this finished already?

God's kingdom doesn't operate that way. The process toward contentment includes surrender, acceptance, discipline, and trust. It uncovers hidden desires and opens up the secret kingdoms of the soul.

Contentment is gained as I experience life and recognize I have a choice in my response. The value of contentment becomes clearer as I understand discontent—its causes, disguises, and lies. And I can finally achieve contentment when I realize it is a state of being with which I clothe my spirit, an attitude that I can wear in any circumstance.

I invite you to join me in this quest of discovery. Together, let's look at God's Word and learn to embrace "enough" and resist the overindulgence of our culture. Let's learn to accept what God gives, both gains and losses, and surrender to His plan. Let's adopt a biblical attitude toward prosperity and success. Let's focus on the benefits and blessings that surround us every day. Let's start on that journey to being simply content.

1

God's Benevolence: Blessing or Bling?

Genesis 3:1–6

Every good and perfect gift is from above, coming down
from the Father of the heavenly lights.

—James 1:17

Discovery

God gives good things and the boundaries within which to enjoy
them.

For Openers

As a teenager, I was certain God was going to require me to
become something I didn't like or go somewhere I would
hate. Over the years, I had heard people in the church relate
stories of the unappealing things God had asked them to do and
how they struggled long and hard over the surrender, but finally
found peace and even joy when they gave in.

Perhaps I got the notion that God usually requires the undesirable because rarely do people give a testimony of how God called them to do something they love. I guess the other type of scenario makes for better storytelling. Where is the struggle in accepting something pleasing?

I've found that quite a few people have a similar misconception. The belief that God is a cosmic killjoy is widespread. To many, it seems God is more a taker of good things than a giver. And when He does send blessings, He probably does it a bit grudgingly, preferring us to endure hardship than enjoy benefits.

Now, it is true that God asks for first place in our hearts, period. Whenever we set our minds on something we must have at all costs, God will be sure to ask us to give it to Him. And that's the important, untold line in those testimonies I heard. Remember the story of the rich young ruler in Luke 18?

If we are to believe the Bible, our God is characterized by generosity. From the beginning of the human story, God gave good things; very good things. In fact, He planned this whole world for our enjoyment. Imagine! But with His blessings, He gives boundaries. With His gifts come guidelines. And that is something no human has been able to stay within, beginning with the first couple. It all started when they doubted His benevolence and wisdom.

Getting to Know Her

Once upon a time, there was a woman who lived a perfectly happy life. Her home, neighborhood, husband, appearance—they were all flawless. She had a good job, was never sick, and enjoyed a marriage actually made in heaven. And on top of all that, her evening walking companion was God. That's right, God—Creator, Master of the universe, Jehovah. He was the one who gave her all these things.

But, she had an Enemy. He was determined to find a way to infiltrate her perfect existence. He couldn't have actually known how her mind worked, but being crafty, he didn't give up easily. He set his eyes on her vulnerability—her reasoning powers and ability to choose.

Read **Genesis 3:1-6**. One day when Eve was walking in her gorgeous garden, his chance came. No marketing associate ever created a better hook. He merely suggested to her that there might be more—more to life, more for her. Sure, God had set boundaries, but maybe He was actually withholding something she needed, something that would make her life better. Well, you know the story; she bit—literally.

But, the fruit that dangled so beautifully before her eyes had a bitter taste. And instead of more, she had less. Sin never gives; it always takes.

It's amazing, isn't it, that a woman who knew nothing but perfection could even be tempted with the thought of having more. What inner compulsion drew her toward a feeling of desire, even lust? In her perfect state, how did she even know a feeling other than satisfaction?

The answer must lie in the human psyche. Created by a genius God, we bear His image in our small way. We must resemble Him in the ability to visualize something wonderful that is not yet reality. If He could imagine our galaxy and babies' smiles and DNA, why can't we dream up the fantastic emotion of having something that promises happiness?

The serpent appealed to her naturally inquisitive mind; he zeroed in on her love of knowledge. She got into trouble because she allowed her curiosity to go beyond the limits of her understanding. Rather than trust the wisdom of her loving creator and friend, she began to believe that He was holding out on her. She let herself imagine how indulgence would taste. And that's all it took for sin to slither into our world.

From then until now, every one of us has struggled with a wrong perception of God, our Father in heaven, who loves to give, but always with boundaries.

The Word Speaks

There is a popular saying that God cares more about making us holy than making us happy. That is true in the purest sense. Yet, there is danger in embracing the belief that deprivation leads to a holy life. That way of thinking is called *asceticism*.

Down through history, asceticism has been embraced by various groups: a few early Christian sects, religious systems such as yoga and Buddhism, and various Monastic orders. Some adhere to the doctrine more strictly than others, but the root belief is the same—austerity of lifestyle promotes spiritual gain. In fact, monks and nuns of some religious orders search for ways in which to deny themselves ordinary creature comforts and care of the body.

The reformer, Martin Luther, a former Augustinian monk, knew the harshness of the ascetic lifestyle. Before he understood justification by faith, he sought God's favor by inflicting pain on his body, abstaining from food, depriving himself of sleep, and exposing himself to severe cold by lying naked on the monastery floor. But nothing eased his guilt.

Throughout the church ages, there has been the need to guard against asceticism as a means to God's grace. But any serious student of the Bible cannot deny the principle of restraint found in its teaching. There are warnings against gluttony, lust, and other types of wrongful indulgence.

The founder of Methodism, John Wesley, adhered to practices that he saw as the natural outflow of the disciplined life. He lived in a rather Spartan manner, but his

What Others Say

Wesley's rationale for simple living is that the gratification of our desires inevitably results in the growth of those very same desires. In gratifying our sensual desires, we find that our sensual desires become stronger and more varied. In gratifying our desire for beautiful things, we find that desire growing stronger (Wesley refers to it as "curiosity"). When we indulge our vanity, our vanity grows.

—Delmar E. Searls

simplicity and frugality were the methods he adopted as borders for his spiritual well-being.

Read Luke 21:34. In talking of His return, Jesus told His followers to be on their guard against the kind of indulgence that places one's focus on this earth. The tone carries the sense of "too full or excess." The principle seems to be that lives crammed with earthly gratification lead to carelessness in spiritual matters.

Notice also Ephesians 5:18 where Paul exhorted his readers not to indulge any appetite without restraint, but to be under the control of the Holy Spirit.

For balance, look at 1 Timothy 4:3 where Paul counseled his son in the faith to beware of those who came teaching mandatory celibacy and abstinence from certain foods as though they were biblical commands. He said such teachings are the "doctrines of devils" (4:1 KJV). Since God is the giver of good things, it cannot be accurate that we must abstain from His gifts in order to be holy. Clearly, the core of ascetic teaching is in violation of the Bible.

Now read Ecclesiastes 3:12–13. Solomon, the wise man, said that food and drink and enjoying the benefits of honest labor are God's gifts.

Turn to Matthew 7:7–11. Jesus taught that the generosity of earthly fathers cannot even be compared with that of our Father in heaven. Think about how you feel when you are able to give your child a much longed-for gift. Why do we have difficulty believing that God delights in giving His children good things? What does this tell us about our view of Him?

Now look at Psalm 103:1–5. In speaking of God's blessings, the psalmist used the imagery of eating something delicious and satisfying. Why do you think we sometimes visualize God's gifts as unpalatable? What might it tell us about our appetites?

Where We Come In

So, what is the balance here? How do we reconcile the themes of God's generosity and Christian restraint?

> ### Bible Background
>
> Fish and bread were the common food of the peasants of Galilee. A stone might resemble a cake, but if given it would deceive the child. A serpent might resemble an eel or a perch, but if given it would be both deceptive and injurious. We often misunderstand God's answer thus. But our sense of sonship should teach us better.
>
> —*The Fourfold Gospel*

Like any good father, God takes no joy in depriving His children. He delights in bestowing blessings and observing our happiness.

But also like a good father, He knows that we don't truly need everything that looks good to us. He gives gifts based on His wisdom, not ours.

The word *bling* is a slang term for adornment that is flashy or ostentatious. It carries the feeling

> ### What Others Say
>
> The comforts of life come from God, as well as the necessaries. He not only gives us a bare subsistence, but he gives us enjoyments.
>
> —Adam Clarke

of something excessive. Sometimes we want things that God sees as bling. He knows it's not good for us. He desires to give us blessings—things that will enrich our lives and not have a negative effect on our relationship with Him. He doesn't give bling—indulgence without restraint. He gives blessing—gifts with responsibility.

God created good things for our enjoyment. He gives us the ability to sense satisfaction. He also gives us boundaries to indulgence. Trusting His judgment and believing in His goodness are the first steps on the pathway of contentment.

How It Works Today

Raised in a preacher's home, Karen learned early about Jesus' love and Christian service. Her parents were dedicated believers, serving small congregations at personal financial sacrifice. In a home blessed with a caring family, Karen didn't feel deprived, but as she grew older, she realized the monetary struggles her family had faced in ministry situations. She promised herself that, when it was her turn to be a parishioner, she would be sure her pastor and family were well cared for. God favored Karen with a solid Christian husband and three terrific children to raise, but she didn't forget her vow. When her kids were older, Karen returned to college for training in the medical field. As she received financial benefits in her new vocation, Karen offered them back to God through generous gifts to her pastor's family. Whether it was a needed home appliance or new clothes and shoes for the children or an unexpected treat at Dairy Queen, she delighted in being God's channel for providing true blessing to a family in Christian service. Because of Karen's kindness, people could see in living color that the heavenly Father gives "good things" to enjoy.

Responding through Prayer

Imagine a beautiful Christmas tree surrounded by gifts with your name on the tags. The tree is your life. The gifts are blessings you have already been given and those you will receive in the future— your physical life, the relationships you have, and the stuff you enjoy. Standing beside the tree with a gentle smile on His face is your heavenly Father.

What would you say to Him as you survey the tangible evidence of His benevolence? Say it to Him now in a quiet prayer.

My Next Step

Bling looks so good. Blessing sometimes comes in disguise. This week, I will be on the lookout for God's goodness to me by:

- Noticing the sheer delights of being alive—vibrant colors, incredible sounds, delicious tastes, and more.
- Recognizing the extra pleasures I enjoy everyday—coffee in the morning, books on the nightstand, dinner at a restaurant, and other small joys.
-
-

Keep It in Mind

Our Father loves us too much to give us bling, but He enjoys giving us blessing. "Trust in . . . the living God, who gives us richly all things to enjoy" (1 Tim. 6:17 NKJV).

2

Divas, Addictions, and Idols

Genesis 19:15–26

*The eye never has enough of seeing,
nor the ear its fill of hearing.*

—Ecclesiastes 1:8

Discovery

Greed is a consuming lust for unrestricted indulgence; the Bible
calls it idolatry.

For Openers

Calling your girlfriend a *diva* probably won't offend her; it's
considered cute, even complimentary. But, is it really?

There are "diva" T-shirts in all colors, some in pink with scrolling
font, some with leopard print background, some with metallic
lettering, and some for little girls proclaiming "Diva in Training"

or "When I grow up, I'm going to be a fashion diva like my aunt!"

The word *diva* was originally used to describe a female opera singer (similar to a prima donna), a leading lady. Maybe because of the temperamental nature of musicians, it also came to denote an imperious, self-absorbed manner. And today, in urban language, it means a woman who will do almost anything to get what she wants. A diva always gets her way.

Most of the time, we don't mean it like that. We like the exotic flair of the word and the sense of affirmation it seems to hold. Maybe we wouldn't use it so freely if we understood that it represents an attitude of self-indulgence that can be detrimental to God's work in us.

Getting to Know Her

Do you remember the story of King Midas? If so, you know that the story ends when, because of his greed, he inadvertently turns his own daughter into a golden statue—hard, cold, and lifeless. God's Word tells the story of a woman who also became a statue, not of gold, but of salt.

Read **Genesis 19:15-26**. She lived in the center of luxury of her day. Sodom and Gomorrah were part of a group referred to as the "cities of the plain." They were well-watered, lush, and rich in natural resources. Genesis 13:10 compares them to "the garden of the LORD." Unfortunately, these cities were also centers of wickedness, rampant with gross sexual perversions. And the behavior of the inhabitants became so offensive to God that He decided to destroy them.

God sent angels to escort Lot and his entire family out of the city, but it was only Lot, his wife, and two unmarried daughters who escaped the doomed cities. God sent catastrophic destruction upon them, either through a volcanic eruption, lightning strike, or some other supernatural means that "rained down burning sulfur" (Gen. 19:24) on all who remained there.

> **Bible Background**
>
> The dale of Siddim, in which the cities were, appears to have abounded in asphalt and other combustible materials (Gen. 14:10). The district was liable to earthquakes and volcanic eruptions from the earliest to the latest times.
>
> —Albert Barnes

The Bible tells us little about Lot's wife. She is mentioned only twice. Both times, she is remembered for desiring what had been forbidden. Genesis 19:26 says that she looked back at the burning cities, disobeying God's express command, and became a pillar (statue) of salt.

God wants us to note her sin. She put higher value on things (her possessions and way of life) than God's will. Her look back was an indication of what held her affections. In doing this, she aligned herself with those in the city who prized their own desires above God and therefore shared in their punishment.

No doubt her story had become legendary in the Jewish community. In Luke 17:32, Jesus referred to her in His teaching. All He needed to say was, "Remember Lot's wife!" She was a tragic symbol of the fact that valuing things above God leads to disaster.

The Word Speaks

Remember Eve and her perfect world? Have you ever considered that she was tempted to indulge in forbidden fruit *before* the blight of sin had entered our world? How can that be?

Read Genesis 3:6. What are the two reasons named that Eve took the fruit?

Usually, we think of Eve's sin in terms of rebellion. And it certainly was. But what prompted her to rebel? Did she merely decide to do her own thing or was there another motivation?

Appetite can be generally defined as a desire or liking for something, a fondness, or taste. Humans have many appetites, involuntary cravings that of themselves are not sinful but rather neutral. They are simply part of the human experience. But the Bible indicates that Eve allowed her natural appetites to overrule her commitment to obedience.

Read the quote by Charles Finney in the sidebar. Eve's hunger, both for food and for knowledge, was the appetite to which Satan appealed. In and of themselves, these desires were harmless. The sin was in the way she chose to gratify them. John Calvin once

What Others Say

Here is nothing of a craving for sin. Eating this fruit was indeed sinful; but the sin consisted in consenting to gratify, in a prohibited manner, the appetites, not for sin, but for food and knowledge. . . . This led to prohibited indulgence. But all men sin in precisely the same way. They consent to gratify, not a craving for sin, but a craving for other things, and the consent to make self-gratification an end, is the whole of sin.

—Charles G. Finney

said, "The evil in our desire typically does not lie in what we want, but that we want it too much."[1]

We do not know the battle in Eve's mind before she sinned. We must not imagine that she cared little for God or took His commands lightly. But, in the end, she valued the fulfillment of her desire above God's command. And Adam did the same.

Now read Matthew 4:1–11. Jesus Christ was fully human and fully divine. Matthew tells us that He was hungry; He had normal human appetites. Satan used that avenue to tempt Him to sinful indulgence. In verses 6 and 9, he appealed to other channels of Jesus' humanity—the desire for affirmation (miracle protection), luxury, and ease (the kingdoms of the world, avoiding the cross).

Jesus refused to consider Satan's suggestions. He was surrendered to the will of the Father above the fulfillment of His human desires.

Where We Come In

Read 1 John 2:15–17. The apostle John warned us against adopting the world's value system. The word translated "lust" or "desire" indicates those feelings of greed that dominate our culture. Many people spend their entire lives consumed with an appetite for things they believe will fill the hunger inside them. But in the end, John said the world and its monstrous greed will pass away. Only those who make the will of God their chief desire will abide forever.

Discontent begins when we allow the satisfaction of our human appetites to become our focus. Like Eve, we will be confronted with the temptation to covet what we have not been given. And the Bible calls greed a form of idolatry.

At its core, sin is greed—indulging our human desires outside of God's provisions. This elevates our desires to a place of prominence over God. Whatever is supreme in our life instead of God is an idol.

Charles Dickens painted the classic image of greed in his famous miserly character, Ebenezer Scrooge. "Oh! But he was a tight-fisted hand at the grindstone, Scrooge! a squeezing, wrenching, grasping, scraping, clutching, covetous, old sinner!"[2] What an ugly portrait! Yet, we do not imagine that we could ever be like that.

But the Bible teaches that idolatry is valuing anything more highly than God. And from the beginning of time, humans have been apt to do just that.

What Others Say

The first two—lust of the flesh and lust of the eyes—refer to desires for what we don't have. And the third—the pride of life—refers to the pride in what we do have. The world is driven by these two things: passion for pleasure and pride in possessions. . . . Anything that is not God can draw your heart away from God. If you don't have it, it can fill you with passion to get it. If you get it, it can fill you with pride that you've got it.

—John Piper

What Others Say

Every one of us is, even from his mother's womb, a master craftsman of idols.

—John Calvin

Read Colossians 3:1–5. Idolatry is a perversion of worship. Look at Paul's words to the Colossian believers. "So kill (deaden, deprive of power) . . . all greed and covetousness, for that is idolatry (the deifying of self and other created things instead of God)" (Col. 3:5 AMP).

When self's appetites become the focus and passion of our lives, who are we actually worshiping?

Turn to Mark 4:18–19. These verses are from Jesus' parable about the soil. Look carefully at the list of things that can choke or strangle the life of God in our hearts—the demands of daily living, the lure or false promises of accumulating wealth, and the desire for "other things."

That last phrase is rather a catch-all statement where Jesus addressed all the human desires that can grow out of proportion and take over our lives like weeds overrun a garden. The word translated "lust" or "desire" is the Greek word *epithumiai* which means a neutral desire. It can indicate a yearning for something either positive or negative.

This tells us that even a normally legitimate desire can become an idol in our lives if it displaces our priorities, if it keeps Him from holding first place. Our natural human appetites (for happiness, relationship, pleasure, comfort, food, sex) that involuntarily beg fulfillment and satisfaction have the potential to become renegade monsters if fed on a diet of self-centeredness rather than surrender to the Spirit. And once given supremacy in our lives, they can never be satisfied. We weren't designed to be devoted to them, but to God. They can't satisfy us; all they can do is demand more. When we gorge ourselves on the fulfillment of our own desires, we are always left hungrier than before. Addiction is the behavior of an idolater.

Read 1 Corinthians 6:9–12. In the pagan city of Corinth, there was a growing congregation of people who had been delivered from addictions of every kind. Notice that idolaters are named in the list. But each of these sins can be cleansed by the blood of Christ, and the Corinthian Christians were living examples of that fact. After being delivered from the addictions, they were not to live under the power of their human appetites, but rather in the fulfillment of a relationship with Christ.

Did You Know?

We can take anything, most of which are good things, perfectly good gifts that God gave us to enjoy—pleasure and friends and houses and real estate and marriage and sex and kids and ministry and jobs and all good gifts that God gives—and we turn them into idols. . . . Idolatry is rarely a bad thing, it's usually a good thing elevated to a God thing which is an evil.

—Mark Driscoll

How It Works Today

For Liz, a pastor's wife with small children, idolatry was an irrelevant concept. Raised in church and saved at a tender age, she had known and loved the Christian way for many years. Now married to a dedicated pastor and deeply involved in the ministry of their local church, Liz had a life that revolved around biblical principles. But God began bringing new truth to her as she studied His Word and listened to teaching on the subject of idolatry. She discovered that anyone can have idols (and most of us do). They are those things we turn to for comfort, security, and affirmation; they are the places of refuge to which we run, the "saviors" we select for ourselves. As she opened her heart, God deepened her understanding, and she has found her relationship with Christ enriched in new ways. Now she uses what she has learned to challenge others to unearth the idols in their hearts and discover the joy found in giving to Him an undivided love.

Think about the common addictions in our culture. Now, recall the images you've seen today (commercials, billboards, advertising slogans) that encourage greed in these areas. In what ways can a Christian woman guard her heart from the sin of idolatry?

Responding through Prayer

Father, I don't want to let other things choke out Your life in me. My desire is that You be my supreme delight and prize. Reveal to me the idols I have erected to give me pleasure and security. I surrender my appetites to You and ask that You would help me trust You to fill them. In Jesus' name. Amen.

My Next Step

This week, I will examine my heart for idols by:

- Determining what I run to when I need comfort and security.
- Observing the pleasures where I am more likely to overindulge.
-
-

Keep It in Mind

Diva doesn't sound as ugly as idolater, but when the desires of self are the focus, they are identical in meaning. Ditch the diva routine today and let Christ, not self, rule your little kingdom. "Dear children, keep yourselves from idols" (1 John 5:21).

3

It Isn't Chic to Compare

Psalm 78; Jeremiah 3:20

Let your conduct be without covetousness;
be content with such things as you have.

—Hebrews 13:5 NKJV

Discovery

Comparison breeds covetousness that will sabotage contentment.

For Openers

Do you want to ruin a perfectly good day? Buy a fashion magazine in the checkout line, grab an iced mocha, and spend the afternoon looking at what you "should" be.

Jennifer Strickland knows all about those magazine photo-spreads. A former supermodel, she was named the "face of the 90's" by legendary Nina Blanchard. Jen began doing fashion shows at the age of eight and entered the professional modeling world upon graduation from high school, moving to Europe where she walked the runway for Giorgio Armani. She also appeared as Barbie on the doll's thirty-fifth anniversary in Italy, starred in television commercials, and appeared on the covers of magazines such as *Vogue*, *Glamour*, and *Cosmopolitan*. At the age of twenty-three, Jen's life was transformed by the amazing love of Christ, and He gave her a whole new career. Today, Jen is a happy wife and mom and enjoys ministering to women through writing and speaking.

I've read Jen's fascinating book, *Girl Perfect* (Excel Books, 2008), detailing her journey of understanding beauty and its value. She is upfront about the pressures of the fashion world, not just on the market, but also on the models. Comparison is the name of the game. She tells about the fierce competition and jealousy among the girls whose jobs as well as sense of worth depend on their looks. Contentment? Not one of them dares feel happy with herself; there's always the fear of losing your edge and being replaced; there's always a new girl who has something you don't.

Getting to Know Her

The descendants of Abraham are referred to as God's beloved; He is imaged as the ever-faithful husband, protecting and cherishing. Throughout the scriptural record, the sins of Israel are referred to in terms of relationship—prostitution, adultery, wantonness, and unfaithfulness.

Like a promiscuous woman, Israel flirted with what God called other "lovers." What He had done for her was not enough. What

He had given her was not enough. Who He is was not enough. She wanted to be like the other kingdoms. She was never content for long. And her longing for other things took her away from Him and brought disaster upon the nation.

Look at the verses in **Psalm 78** and then read **Jeremiah 3:20**. Think about the many times the nation of Israel complained to the prophet, God's spokesman. Whether it was water or fresh meat or a king like other nations, they always wanted something else. Rarely were they satisfied. Psalm 78 contains a litany of Israel's grievances against God.

Whether it be an individual or a nation, Satan knows how easily persuaded we are—how susceptible to false messages. He used it on Israel, and he uses it on us: "See? This is what you really need. This will make you happy!"

The Word Speaks

Turn to Luke 12:15. Look carefully at the first part of the verse. "And [Jesus] said to them, Guard yourselves and keep free from all covetousness" (AMP).

Look up the word *covet* in a dictionary. Notice that while it can have a negative meaning, it may also simply mean a strong wish, a longing—as in a coveted award. It means wanting something I don't have.

Read Exodus 20:17. This is the tenth item in the list we call the Ten Commandments. Growing up, this was one I never worried about; I hardly even grasped the meaning. As an adult, I see how significant this particular command is.

God told His people not to wish for what belonged to someone else. In other words, don't look at what you have and then at what someone else has and wish for something different.

As women, this one hits us pretty hard. Our culture never fails to present an ideal with which we can compare ourselves. Does this have any relevance for what I feel when I look at the glossy images of women whose beauty and glamour I long to own? Am I trying to be like them? Do I want the admiration they have?

> ## What Others Say
>
> It is God's desire that you reflect His image in the world, not the image of the world.
>
> —Jennifer Strickland

The fashion world thrives on covetousness, dissatisfaction, and greed. Who decides what is beautiful today anyway? Who profits when I accept their definition of beauty? What about home design catalogs and shopping malls? Am I feeding the parasite of greed when I spend hours with them? Can I regularly fill my eyes with their lustrous images and be happy with what God has given me?

Where We Come In

Satan wants to keep us focused on ourselves, and he often works the comparison game. He has done his best to infiltrate the media and marketing world and use it for his purposes.

If I were to ask one thousand American women what makes them most unhappy, what do you think it would be? That's a no-brainer, right? Any woman exposed to Western culture is dissatisfied with her body. When you talk about beauty today, the first thing most women think of is their shape.

And though we know the truth—unhealthy body weights and digital enhancement give the models on posters and magazine covers an advantage over us real-life girls—we still struggle. The knowledge that it's a fantasy doesn't make us more content.

Keeping us dissatisfied with who we are and what we have means we can never fully devote ourselves to God because we're always focused on us, not Him. That's what an obsession with fashion magazines will do—keep us focused on ourselves, our appearance, and our flaws and how they affects our relationships. They foster in us a sense of discontent with who we are.

The *Official Journal of the American Association of Pediatrics* reported on a study done with 548 girls in grades five through twelve. Among those participating, "69 [percent] reported that magazine pictures influence their idea of the perfect body shape, and 47 [percent] reported wanting to lose weight because of magazine pictures."[1] The article went on to report, "This discontentment was strongly related to the frequency of reading fashion magazines. Although previous studies have concluded that the print media promotes an unrealistically thin body ideal, which in turn is at least partially responsible for promoting eating disorders, the present study is the first that we are aware of to assess directly the impact of the print media on the weight and body shape beliefs of young girls."[2]

A credible scientific journal confirms what we already know: comparing ourselves with images of unrealistic beauty makes us

What Others Say

It is essential for Christian girls and women to accept their bodies as creations of God and seek a healthy lifestyle, not a skinny body. . . . For the Christian, personal acceptance is a spiritual matter. We must be willing to receive from God His plan for our lives. We must believe that He always has our best interest in mind. The Bible teaches about acceptance.

—Dr. Rhonda H. Kelley

Comparison can sometimes take on a spiritual tone. Christian women can get caught up in the game of measuring their spiritual progress or spiritual gifts by the women in their small group or church. Satan tweaks the settings a little bit, but the result is the same—contentment is nonexistent when I begin comparing myself with others.

discontent. And those feelings don't disappear after twelfth grade. While adult women may have the maturity to realize their worth isn't solely related to their looks, the message is still potent among the college-aged, young moms, and grandmothers. Comparison exerts its powerful force upon us every day.

What Others Say

A blogger who goes by "Fiona" wrote the following in a post titled "On Contentment," posted on her blog, "How to Be Chic":

"Be mindful of what you read. I often feel dissatisfied with my own life when I read glossy magazines, 'show-off' blogs and peruse luxury brand websites."

Comments from her readers included:

"It's good to be choosey and discerning by what we let our eyes see . . . which always leads to the heart's desires."

"I'd rather set my own standards than to have a teenage, malnourished model tell me what is hot."

How It Works Today

As a Christian woman, Jody was concerned that she wasn't like her friends. She noticed the obvious joy they exhibited during worship songs and wondered why she was different. Her own sense of exhilaration came from listening to biblical teaching, digging into the Word, and discovering new truths. She loved lexicons and etymology studies, but she felt "un-spiritual" and inferior when she compared herself to the beatific smiles and verbal praise styles of others. God used a series of epiphanies to reveal to Jody that her specific temperament was His design. To her amazement, she realized that her love of study was just as worshipful in His eyes as others' hands being raised in praise. God confirmed this insight to her soon after when her research into a biblical matter helped good friends who were facing a difficult situation and praying for direction. Through this, He showed her that embracing the gifts He had given her would bring fulfillment to her and blessing to others. Jody has found freedom to be the woman God had in mind all along, and with it a new joy. She knows without a doubt that worship is lifting up to Him the best of what you have and are. And knowing He is pleased helps her resist the temptation to compare and continue the journey toward contentment.

How do I tell the difference between a legitimate need for change and a feeling of discontent?

There will always be the need for the transforming power of Christ at work in us. It is important to recognize this. But the Holy Spirit is faithful to show us clearly where we need to allow Him to change us. He never fills us with a sense of despair about the things we see in ourselves—"I'll never be pretty enough; I'll never be able to have a house like that."

Instead, He points out the problem and tells us how to fix it. "Let Me help you with self-control so you can maintain a healthy weight. Let Me help you with your priorities so you can organize your home. Let Me help you with money management so you can buy the dining room table you want."

If you feel hopeless about something, it's probably not the Spirit of God speaking to you. He always gives light that shows the way out. And He never encourages us to compare ourselves with a standard other than the beauty of Jesus.

Responding through Prayer

Creator God, thank you for making me in Your image and thank you for sending Jesus to restore Your likeness in me through His redemptive work on Calvary. Show me how to accept and embrace what You've given me—my body, personality, and gifts—for Your glory. I ask You to continue conforming me to the image of Your Son, and let me see my inadequacies as steps to greater dependence on You. In Jesus' name. Amen.

My Next Step

This week I will refuse to compare myself with others in:

- My dress size.

- My decorating abilities.

-

-

Keep It in Mind

God isn't into cookie-cutter comparisons; He values our unique characteristics and gifts. The only standard that interests Him is the image of His Son, and He is ever working to make us more like Him. "Until we all come to such unity in our faith and knowledge of God's Son that we will be mature in the Lord, measuring up to the full and complete standard of Christ" (Eph. 4:13 NLT).

4

Contentment Means a Cross

Luke 1:26–38

LORD, you have assigned me my portion and my cup; you have made my lot secure.

—Psalm 16:5

Discovery

Contentment flows from surrender and acceptance; it reflects the cross.

For Openers

The Statler Brothers won a Grammy award in 1972 for the song "The Class of '57." The last few lines go like this:

And the class of '57 had its dreams,
But living life from day to day is never like it seems.
Things get complicated when you get past eighteen,
But the class of '57 had its dreams.[1]

Country music may not be your preferred genre, but many times, the lyrics are representative of the common experiences of people. This one falls into that category. The song describes the graduates from a senior class in Anytown, USA, and tells what they're doing now—from working at the mill to selling Tupperware. The implication is that most of them wound up doing things they would not have chosen on graduation night. If you've been out of high school for any length of time, you could say the same thing about your graduating class. Despite our grandiose plans, life rarely turns out exactly like we dreamed it would. Those who don't know Christ may not handle the detours well. Those who do fare better, but unless they grasp hold of the concept of acceptance, bitterness will poison their souls.

Getting to Know Her

She lived in an occupied country. Her people were crushed beneath heavy taxation and brutal control. Her family lived in poverty; her hometown was the dump of the area. She was an unmarried teenager who just learned she was pregnant.

This was Mary of Nazareth.

Read **Luke 1:26-38**. The story is so familiar that we scarcely notice the details. But hers was not a pleasant life; it was one of hardship with little hope. Under the foot of Rome, the land of Israel writhed in resentment and privation, longing for deliverance. The families of Nazareth were far from wealthy, and Mary's probably fit that description. The Bible tells us nothing about her physical appearance—she may have been petite or large-boned, fine featured or average, probably with the dusky coloring and hair of the

Bible Background

No man could ever have imagined that an archangel would be commissioned by the God of all creation to visit a village such as Nazareth, situated in a district, the very name of which announced it as a place of the despised Gentiles . . . "district of the pagans."

—James Burton Coffman

Jewish people. The village where she lived was despised; no one expected anything good to come from Nazareth (John 1:46).

God thought it more important that we know about her character. And that was poignantly revealed on an ordinary day when an angel visited her. The message he gave her was the most astonishing news a woman ever received—she was pregnant and still a virgin. Her adolescent mind grappled with this announcement, immediately wondering about the complications wrapped up in such a situation. She asked Gabriel about it, and he reassured her that with God nothing is impossible.

Now look at verse 38. She said, "I am the Lord's servant." This was a statement of submission, of quiet acceptance. She realized, at least partially, that her life would be changed in dramatic ways from that moment forward, but she did not refuse the assignment she had been given. And in her beautiful surrender to the divine plan, she became the first human to welcome Christ to earth.

The Word Speaks

Read Psalm 37:23. I like how the New Living Translation renders this verse: "The LORD directs the steps of the godly. He delights in every detail of their lives."

Wow, what a promise to build your life on! If we are His daughters, He is directing our lives, delighting in every tiny nuance of the journey like a mom is thrilled with the progress of her toddler. All the components of our lives are included here—relationships, family, jobs, health, finances. The Father in heaven oversees it all.

Did You Know?

The word *handmaid* is the feminine form of a word that meant *slave* or *bondservant*. Jamieson-Fausset-Brown Commentary says it means "one subject to the will and wholly at the disposal of another." Look at Genesis 16:1; Ruth 3:9; and 1 Samuel 1:11. In all three of these passages, a woman is referred to by the same word—handmaid. It implies a submissive attitude. In using this word, Mary signified her total surrender to what was asked.

Now read Psalm 16:5. Look at what Elisabeth Elliot says about this verse. "My 'lot' is what happens to me—my share of that which comes by the will of the Power that rules my destiny. My lot includes the circumstances of my birth, my upbringing, my job, my hardships, the people I work with, my marital status, hindrances, obstacles, accidents, and opportunities. Everything constitutes my lot. Nothing excepted. If I can accept that fact

What Others Say

All his course of life is graciously ordained, and in lovingkindness all is fixed, settled, and maintained. No reckless fate, no fickle chance rules us; our every step is the subject of divine decree.

—*Treasury of David*

45

at every turn of the road, I have indeed stepped into His everlasting arms of joy even more securely, and there I will find peace and joy."[2]

That's a little hard for us to embrace, isn't it? It seems to put a lot of weight on the sovereignty of God. And that's problematic for some of us. Does it detract from the importance of each person's choice?

It's true that many of the factors of our lives are directly related to the choices of others. God will not violate the free will of any person on earth, even if that means he or she makes the choice to cause pain in the life of one of His children. There are times when He chooses to protect His child from the consequences of the other's action; and there are times when He does not—the Bible records examples of both scenarios. Then there are other instances when something comes into our lives, not from human cause, but by divine permission.

Read Job 1:6–22 and 2:1–10. If there is a poster child for sudden catastrophic loss, it's Job. He didn't ask for it or deserve it. In fact, he was living above the standard of anyone else on the earth— that's what God said to Satan in verse 3. But God allowed unbelievably painful circumstances in his life.

Much has been written about Job's attitude, but today, let's focus on his wife. Verse 8 shows us what happens when a woman allows herself to become bitter because God "disappoints" her or because life isn't what she'd planned.

To be fair, Job's wife did suffer overwhelming tragedy in a short amount of time. All of her children were dead in the space of a few minutes, her wealth was obliterated, and her husband—the man whom she needed to be her comfort and protection—was stricken with horrible infected ulcers on his skin and was so depressed that all he could do was sit in the ashes (literally and figuratively) and scrape his sores. Talk about bad! That's off the charts.

But instead of turning *to* God for strength, she turned *against* Him in rage. The only God she could trust was one who allowed things she liked. When He asked her to trust Him in the unpleasant times, she couldn't. Fuming at God and disgusted with Job, she said to him, "Are you still trying to maintain your integrity? Curse God and die" (2:9 NLT).

Look at Job's answer: "You talk like a foolish woman. Should we accept only good things from the hand of God and never anything bad?" (2:10 NLT). Now, he wasn't without feeling. Later chapters tell us Job mourned, was angry, and questioned God about his trials, but he trusted the divine character of God, and that gave him a different perspective than his wife.

Like Job, the important thing for us to remember is that whatever comes into our lives, by His direct act or by the choice He allowed someone else to make, is part of the path He has appointed. Both the negative and the positive can be used for good if consecrated to Him.

We must hold God's blessings with open hands. They are not ours to clutch; they are His to give and remove as He knows is best. As Abraham laying his beloved son on the altar, we must be willing to give them back to Him. Embracing this perspective gives us power over idolatry because it is built on love for God and trust

What Others Say

To those of us who are not theologians, does it matter whether a thing is ordained or merely allowed? Are events that seem to be out of control caused by God? Or does He allow them to occur at the hands of human beings? You can spend a lot of time pondering that one and end up pretty much where you started. In either case, the purpose remains the same—our sanctification. God is in the business of making us walking, breathing examples of the invisible reality of the presence of Christ in us.

—Elisabeth Elliot

in His character, which means that we place the supreme value on who He is rather than on what He gives. "In other words, if created things are seen and handled as gifts of God and as mirrors of His glory, they need not be occasions of idolatry—if our delight in them is always also a delight in their Maker."[3] This is the secret of Job's attitude—above all things, he delighted in God (see Job 1;1, 5).

Turn to Romans 8:28–31.These verses have been used so much that many people immediately recoil from them. At times, they have been used to trivialize and ignore real pain that isn't easily fixed. But we cannot ignore the fact that they are God's Words and speak an important truth to this discussion.

Notice some things about this passage. Whose purpose are we called unto? To whose image has God chosen for us to be conformed? Who can be against us?

These verses shout to us that, despite the inconveniences, injustices, and abuses we endure in our lives, nothing can derail God's ultimate plan for us—to make us more and more like Jesus.

Where We Come In

Our response to the unpleasant and painful things in our lives must be the response of Christ—death to our will and acceptance of the Father's. The life that leads us ever onward to Christlikeness is one of ever-deepening surrender. Contentment, not the artificial kind, but the stuff that gleams solid in the tough times, reflects the cross. It is fashioned of surrender.

In one of her poems, Amy Carmichael penned the line, "In acceptance lieth peace."[4]

What Others Say

Life requires countless "little" deaths—occasions where we are given the chance to say no to self and yes to God.

—Elisabeth Elliot

She was right. The companion to surrender is acceptance. The Spirit chooses the path and the places along the way where we must follow blood-stained footprints. If He can suffer so greatly for me, can I not bear this small inconvenience or injustice with an accepting heart?

Do you wish God had fashioned you differently? Do you long for a different house, neighborhood, and job? Do you see flaws in your spouse that seem unfair? Do you feel dissatisfied with what you own? Do you feel unhappy with the complications of this season in your life? This then is the crucible in which you can learn contentment. You are in the perfect place to learn to say, as He did, "Not my will, but Yours be done."

How It Works Today

Becky has learned to trust the Father's assignments in her life. She was raised in a loving Christian home with eight siblings and parents who gave their life and love to ministry. She married a wonderful godly man and settled down into a life in the parsonage. But God called them to the mission field, and they arrived in the Philippines with two small children and another on the way. It was after the birth of their third child that Becky faced a significant challenge to her trust in God and acceptance of His will. At the age of two months, Jesse was diagnosed with retinoblastoma and endured months of treatments and surgeries, eventually losing both eyes to the cancer. Overwhelmed with ministry demands in a foreign country and the care of her special-needs child, Becky fought depression, making conscious choices every day to trust the One who saw the big picture of life from a heavenly perspective. She and her husband Tim continued to minister, seeing God work incredible miracles as He provided for Jesse's health needs in ways that astounded them. After serving the field in Southeast Asia for thirteen years and the addition of two more little girls to their family, they began a new ministry season in the States where Tim became the director of a denominational mission's organization. Again, there were challenges as they readjusted to life in the States and helped Jesse learn to become comfortable in a whole new environment. And the journey isn't over yet, but Becky knows that God will provide enough grace for today and that means she can be content. There is no threat that can dim the shining faithfulness of the Father.

Responding through Prayer

Father, You have seen every detail of my life from the moment I was conceived. You know the losses I've suffered along the way. You know the dreams I had that have not come true. I ask that You would enable me to look ahead with surrender and acceptance. Let me refuse to be bitter and instead choose to be content. In Christ's name. Amen.

My Next Step

Contentment flows from acceptance and surrender. List below some areas of your life where you need to implement this concept:

- My family.

- My health issues.

-

-

Keep It in Mind

In Philippians 4:11, the apostle Paul stated that he had learned to be content. The words *learned* and *be* denote both process and choice. The Greek word translated here as learn is *manthan* ; it means to increase in knowledge, to learn by use and practice, to be in the habit of. There is action and personal initiative involved here. Let's take Paul's words as our lifelong assignment: "I have learned to be content whatever the circumstances. I know what it is to be in need, and I know what it is to have plenty. I have learned the secret of being content in any and every situation, whether well fed or hungry, whether living in plenty or in want" (Phil. 4:11–12).

5

Heroic Husbands, Contented Wives

1 Samuel 18:17–30; 2 Samuel 6:12–21

Bear with each other and forgive whatever grievances you may have against one another. Forgive as the Lord forgave you. And over all these virtues put on love, which binds them all together in perfect unity.

—Colossians 3:13–14

Discovery

I can be content with my husband if I choose not to focus on his imperfections, but look for the hero in him.

For Openers

While this chapter is targeting married women, single women are included here too. If you're single, you're forming opinions that will affect your behavior if God gives you a husband. By learning this lesson now, you can be ahead of the game. And everyone, single or married, needs to understand the concept of accepting the quirks in those we live and work with.

Remember that magical season in your life when you fell in love? Most women have sweet memories of special romantic outings, the night he proposed, and the breathtaking moments leading up to the wedding day.

Maybe you met him in class, at a church event, or at a friend's house; wherever it was, there was some indefinable spark inside that started the whole thing. Probably before he ever asked you out, you were watching him, taking in his voice, build, laugh, and mannerisms. When you started dating, you became more and more intrigued with the way he thought about life, how he solved problems, and his plans for the future. You prized his perspective and opinions; he was the most incredible man on earth to you.

Getting to Know Her

That's what it was like for Michal, in the beginning. Read **1 Samuel 18:17-30**. She was a princess, one of the daughters of King Saul. Her name (pronounced "mee-khal") is the feminine form of Michael and means "who is like God."

Michal was in love. Who wouldn't be with a guy like David? He was a national hero, a military commander, had a gorgeous singing voice, and was extremely good-looking. Beside all that, he had been anointed to be king one day.

She'd almost grieved herself to death when her father started talking about giving her sister Merab to David as a wife (v. 17). But David wondered how someone so poor could marry royalty. Rather than try to convince him, Saul gave his eldest daughter to someone else. But he was determined to use marriage as a way to get rid of David (nice dad, huh?). Michal's dream came true when her dad offered her to the most eligible man in Israel. Saul demanded a dowry, hoping David would be killed trying to collect it. But God protected him, and the wedding took place.

Michal was, no doubt, ecstatic. Though her father hated her new husband, she loved him intensely. When Saul tried again to murder David, Michal helped him escape (19:8–18).

After he fled into the night, things became chaotic in David's life, largely due to Saul's mad lust for his blood. Hiding in caves with a band of men who became his own small army, David was separated from Michal for a long while. Scripture says in 1 Samuel 25:44 that, after a while, Saul gave Michal in marriage to a man named Paltiel.

Eventually, David became the appointed king of Israel. He demanded that Michal be returned to him, which he had every right to do. Michal's second husband was heartbroken. Second Samuel 3:15–16 tells us that Michal was forcibly taken from his home and that he followed after the raiding party, weeping.

Michal was in a situation that had to have been terribly hard. We don't know for sure whether she loved Paltiel or not. Maybe she resented David for taking her from him. Or maybe secretly she still pined for David all those years. In any case, David was still her husband and deserving of her honor. But the next time we read about Michal, her story takes another bitter turn.

Read **2 Samuel 6:12–21**. King David was euphoric. The ark of the covenant, the symbol of God's presence and blessing was coming home. As the procession entered the city, Michal was watching from her window. No doubt she had often watched David in the past, returning triumphant from battle, strong and virile, a man blessed with God's power and presence. Surely, at those times, she had longed to run to him, look adoringly into his face and welcome him home. But this time it was different. Instead of adoration, she felt contempt. She saw him worshiping in a way she considered undignified, not appropriate for a king. She noticed that he had taken off his kingly clothing. She was embarrassed by his behavior, and "she despised him in her heart" (v. 16).

Meanwhile, King David blessed his people; he prayed for them and gave them food. Then he returned to his home to bless his own family and Michal met him on the front steps. She wasn't coming with loving eyes and welcoming arms, but with a sneer and cruel words. She was vicious in her sarcasm, verbally attacking him in public.

David responded with anger (most men do when approached this way!). Basically, he said, "It's not your business. God appointed me king, not your father or anyone from this house. I am celebrating before Him, and if I have to be undignified to do that, so be it."

> ### What Others Say
>
> Proud of her royal extraction, she upbraided her husband for lowering the dignity of the crown and acting more like a buffoon than a king.
>
> —Jamieson-Fausset-Brown Commentary

What did Michal do then? Stomp off? Slam the door? We don't know. But the Bible tells us what happened to her because of her bitterness toward her husband: she had no children. The greatest burden for any woman in that culture was childlessness. The Bible indicates that the reason for Michal's attitude toward her husband was her own pride. She valued her reputation more than her husband. The way he expressed his devotion to God was humiliating to her, and she refused to put aside her personal feelings and respect him.

What Others Say

She acted rather as the daughter of Saul than as the wife of David, and therefore like her father she died, leaving no heir to the throne of Israel.

—Spurgeon Devotional Commentary

Did You Know?

Michal never birthed a child of her own, but she raised the five sons of her older sister, Merab. Read 2 Samuel 21:8. King Saul, Michal's father, had mistreated the Gibeonites. When David came to power, they asked for retribution— seven of Saul's descendants should be executed. David agreed, and five of the ones chosen were Saul's grandsons by Merab whom Michal had apparently adopted or at least raised. As a result of this sad event, she was not only biologically childless, but also bereft of the children she raised as her own.

Once a wife begins protecting her own vanity, disregarding the cost to her husband, the relationship is in trouble. We all must avoid that pitfall. A friend and I had a discussion about how tempting it is for wives to try to "protect" our husbands' reputation when actually we're just trying to protect our own pride. We're afraid of what others might think about our husbands and us for marrying them.

In what ways have you been tempted to allow pride to drive you to disrespect your husband?

The Word Speaks

Michal's story is an extreme example of a wife's inappropriate attitude. Let's look at how the Bible describes the right attitude. Here are some verses that set the bar really high.

Look at how the Amplified Bible lays out the varying aspects of the word respect in Ephesians 5:33: "And let the wife see that she respects and reverences her husband [that she notices him, regards him, honors him, prefers him, venerates, and esteems him; and that she defers to him, praises him, and loves and admires him exceedingly]."

Now look at 1 Peter 3:1–2. The apostle was telling wives how they could influence their husbands toward obedience to God by the way they conduct themselves. Notice the way he described a godly wife's attitude: "When they observe the pure and modest way in which you conduct yourselves, together with your reverence [for your husband; you are to feel for him all that reverence includes: to respect, defer to, revere him—to honor, esteem, appreciate, prize, and, in the human sense, to adore him, that is, to admire, praise, be devoted to, deeply love, and enjoy your husband]" (v. 2 AMP).

This is a staggering definition and one we need to be reminded of often. God wants a wife to be in awe of her husband, to think he is heroic. There are no clauses which excuse women when their husbands don't earn respect, just as there are no exceptions for men not to love their wives because of their flaws. The command for wives to respect and husbands to love is not based on the performance of the spouse.

Where We Come In

Those who expect the fleeting intoxication of a crush to continue are sadly disillusioned with real life. A woman may become discontent with her husband because he's not the man she wishes for or thought he was. And granted, there are things that every spouse needs to work on, especially in the area of relationships. Men aren't perfect; not one of them. We knew that before the wedding, but there is nothing like daily life to prove it! And women—we aren't perfect either. It's important to remember that as well!

Perhaps you wonder if you married out of God's will, and if that is the reason for your struggle. Remember that we're only talking about particular flaws, not the absence of them. If you had married someone else, there would be traits in him that you would wish to change.

When you get right down to it, allowing yourself to be discontent with your husband is harboring an attitude of ungratefulness for what God has given you. The assignment of every wife is to find the hero in her husband. Whatever his age or profession, every man is equipped by God to be a hero, a strong defender and protector. His battleground might be a pulpit or a truck cab, a conference room or a construction site. But he is called to be a warrior for truth, integrity, justice, and honor.

A hero is someone to admire, but no one expects him to be totally perfect. We all have quirks and flaws. Your husband isn't less a hero because of his. What drew you to him in the first place is probably still there. If a wife admires her husband, how might she respond to the less significant faults in him?

Sometimes there are serious relational issues that make dialog necessary. Like David, no man responds well to "mommy" type criticism or belittling accusations, and it is not kind or respectful to address him in that manner. As wives, we need to pay special attention to the words we choose, the tone of voice we use, and the expression of our faces. Husbands are inordinately sensitive in these areas, and they can distinguish disrespect a mile away.

But most of the irritants in marriage are the "little things" that represent only a small portion, and not the whole. Read what Elisabeth Elliot says about this (see sidebar).

What is your reaction to her suggestion? Explain why a spouse, husband or wife, might demand that the other please him or her in every detail.

Read Colossians 3:12–14. Look at the choice implied in verse 12. The NIV says "clothe;" it is something done intentionally. Verse 13 nails the attitude we should have—bear with and forgive (as Christ forgave). If Michal had done this, instead of imposing her prideful expectations on her husband, her story could have been different.

> ### What Others Say
>
> A wife, if she is very generous, may allow that her husband lives up to perhaps 80 percent of her expectations. There is always the other 20 percent that she would like to change, and she may chip away at it for the whole of their married life without reducing it by very much. She may, on the other hand, simply decide to enjoy the 80 percent, and both of them will be happy. It's a down-to-earth illustration of a principle: *Accept, positively and actively, what is given.*
>
> —Elisabeth Elliot

These two ideas go hand in hand: looking for the hero and putting up with flaws. One balances the other. We can't expect a human hero to be perfect, and we can't deny admiration for the big things because of small things. A wife needs to guard her perspective.

Of course, no one should overlook abuse or criminal activity. If you are facing these types of issues, get some guidance from your pastor or a Christian counselor.

If you are unmarried, decide right now to let God guide your choice of a husband and then honor him will all your might if He gives you one. God is in the business of making heroes for women who care enough to discover them.

How It Works Today

Janet has been married over fifty years to the same man. In that amount of time, they have had quite a journey. From newlyweds to missions and evangelism to the pastorate, they have ministered, worshiped, parented, celebrated, and grieved together. Life has given them many opportunities and challenges. In positions of leadership and under the accompanying stress, Janet has observed her husband in many capacities and situations. She knows all the little things no one else does. Yet, her staff in the medical practice where she served as a nurse practitioner believed her husband must be the greatest man on earth. That's because Janet made it her personal policy never to say anything negative about him to them. She honored him and built him up with her words, choosing to make his positive traits her focus, purposefully looking for the hero in him. And through all the twists and turns in their life together, their contentment with each other has made their ministry more credible and their home more delightful. Their story is a witness to the validity of choosing to honor, and because they did, many others around the world have been blessed.

Responding through Prayer

Thank you, Lord, for the husband You've given me. Help me accept him and respect him. Reveal to me the hero You created him to be. Let me show him an attitude of honor and never attack or belittle him. Use me to make our marriage a happy one. In Jesus' name. Amen.

My Next Step

Realizing that my emotions are influenced by my choices, I will honor my husband this week by:

- Refusing to compare him mentally with other husbands I know or men I see.
- Refraining from making negative comments about him to my girlfriends.
-
-

Keep It in Mind

The choice to be content with my husband isn't based on his looks, attitude, or performance. It's a choice to accept him with all his gifts and faults and to focus on the positive aspects of his person and our relationship. It's a purposeful decision to admire and respect. "Love bears up under anything and everything that comes, is ever ready to believe the best of every person, its hopes are fadeless under all circumstances, and it endures everything [without weakening]" (1 Cor. 13:7 AMP).

6

Little House and Happy Hearts

Matthew 20:20–24; Exodus 2:1–10

The godly walk with integrity;
blessed are their children who follow them.

—Proverbs 20:7 NLT

Discovery

A mother can help her children adopt a biblical perspective toward wealth and power.

For Openers

I f you're familiar with the *Little House on the Prairie* books or television series, you know the name Nellie Oleson— nemesis of the main character, Laura Ingalls. Nellie personified what we call the "spoiled child"—bratty, sassy, whiney, greedy, condescending, and basically irritating. And the storyline (of the television series, at least) provides us with a clue as to how she developed these traits—her mother, Mrs. Harriet Oleson. Mrs. Oleson was the sort of woman who didn't just want the best for her children; she wanted them to have better things than anyone else has. We are led to believe that, because of her indulgent and permissive parenting, she encouraged self-centeredness in her daughter.

Mothers are sensitive creatures when it comes to our kids. We protect them; we nurture them; we sacrifice for them. And when they are threatened, we bristle and dash to their defense like a pit bull on a mission.

It is a mother's nature to give—first the gift of life and then everything in her power that will help her children grow and blossom into mature adults. The problem is that at times, it's difficult to distinguish between the essential and superfluous. And that's where Mrs. Oleson made her mistake.

Getting to Know Her

We'll look at two mothers. They represent opposite sides of this discussion.

Read **Matthew 20:20-24**. Commentators say her name was Salome, the wife of Zebedee, the mother of James and John. She came to Jesus with a request. Some biblical scholars believe that it was, in fact, James and John who wished to ask this favor of Jesus and had their mother do it on their behalf. Perhaps they were ashamed to ask such a thing or they hoped their mother would have better success, since it is believed she was Jesus' aunt.

If the idea originated with her sons, it reveals their greedy hearts, true. But, as their mother, it was her responsibility to help them see their error. And certainly, she should have refused to be their spokesperson. Salome may not have realized all the implications of this request, but she knew she was asking for special treatment or special favors in regard to her children. And that is almost always detrimental.

Now, read the story in **Exodus 2:1-10**. Here we are introduced to the deliverer, the lawgiver—Moses. His mother's name was Jochebed (Num. 26:59). This woman came from the priestly line, as did her husband. The Bible doesn't give us many other details about her, but her actions show that she was a woman of strong faith, courage, and wisdom.

Moses was likely born just after Pharaoh's decree that all male Hebrew babies were to be killed. Jochebed hid him somehow until he was three months old, and then created a little waterproof boat and put him into the reedy bank of the Nile, with his older sister keeping watch over him.

Biblical scholars have speculated various reasons why Pharaoh's daughter came to the Nile that day, but whatever it was, she and her servant girls were walking by the river when she saw the odd little basket. She sent her personal maid to get it and when she opened it, the baby began to cry. And she fell in love with the beautiful infant boy inside.

Because she saw he was circumcised, she knew immediately that he was Hebrew. But that didn't matter to her. When Miriam sidled up and offered to find a wet nurse, she accepted. Miriam, of course, ran to find her mother. And that's how Jochebed was paid to take care of her own baby! Probably, she was even excused from the heavy slave labor, since she was caring for the princess' adopted son.

Bible Background

The occasion is thought to have been a religious solemnity which the royal family opened by bathing in the sacred stream. Peculiar sacredness was attached to those portions of the Nile which flowed near the temples. The water was there fenced off as a protection from the crocodiles; and doubtless the princess had an enclosure reserved for her own use, the road to which seems to have been well known to Jochebed.

—Jamieson-Faussett-Brown
Commentary

Jochebed was free to delight in her son until he was old enough to wean. Scripture doesn't tell us specifically at what age this would take place, but it was probably between the ages of three and five. In the precious time she had, Jochebed filled her son's little ears with reverence for Yahweh. When she sat nursing him, while he played on the floor, as she lay him down to sleep, she talked to him of the one with whom there was a covenant, the one who would send a deliverer. She told him that he was Hebrew and always would be.

Perhaps Pharaoh's daughter came often to visit or had Jochebed bring the baby to the palace to see her. She was anxious to have her "son." And though Jochebed must have tried to delay the weaning process, at last it was complete, and the time had come to deliver him to the princess.

How must Jochebed have felt handing over her toddler to a pagan Egyptian princess? Though this woman could provide her little boy with a luxurious home and the best education, how would her false religious practices affect him? Would he remember the God who saved him from Pharaoh's sword? As Jochebed let go of his tiny fingers, she must have felt her heart breaking. Even his identity was changed; his new "mother" named him Moses, meaning drawn from the water.

But, Jochebed didn't give up. As mothers, sometimes we feel the odds are too great for our children, but they are never too much for God.

Tell about a time when God protected your child from physical or spiritual harm.

The Word Speaks

Turn to Hebrews 11:23–26. Moses is listed in the Bible's hall of faith. How did he merit this mention? He chose eternal riches over temporal ones. He was not greedy for earthly luxury. He had the proper perspective of wealth and prestige. The court of Pharaoh would not have been the place to learn an attitude of restraint. Is it possible that Jochebed's teachings took root in his small heart and grew until his mature mind could comprehend the choice that was his?

Examine Acts 7:20–23. Moses was educated in all the ways of the Egyptians. Bible commentaries say this means he had been instructed in the subjects in which they excelled—science, medicine, arithmetic, music, astronomy, astrology, and religion. How old does verse 23 say Moses was when he identified himself with the Hebrews?

Think how the nation of Israel would have suffered had Moses been anxious to have his own monument in the Valley of the Kings? What if personal advancement and wealth had been his chief goal? Somehow, Jochebed was able to instill principles in her son that helped him make wise choices later. As mothers, we must help our children adopt appropriate standards with which to measure success.

Read Proverbs 10:1. How Jochebed would have delighted in the discretion of her son as he chose to identify himself with the people of God! As a child, he had been taught to distinguish real value. As a man, his decision would have made his mother proud.

Where We Come In

To a mother is given the chief responsibility for teaching her children many needed skills for life. Besides training them to make their beds, use their dinner napkins, and say please and thank you, it is her obligation to guide them in the proper attitudes that make for a happy life. She must pass on to them the proper perspective of wealth and ambition so that wherever God leads them in adulthood, they may discern what is really valuable.

One way a mother can do this is by the way she responds to the family's financial situation. If they are prosperous, she must not focus on their wealth, displaying it for others' benefit and constantly worrying about status. If they are struggling, she must not blame her husband or God or exude the feeling that the lack of money is making them all miserable. Her attitude toward affluence or hardship has a great bearing on her children.

Describe the philosophy illustrated to Salome's sons by her actions.

In this area of training, we face a great challenge. Our culture prizes gain and success. As mothers, we must help our children see beyond the surface. We must give them a bedrock layer of principle that keeps them centered as they enter a society focused on personal gratification.

How It Works Today

Sherry is a godly woman who mothered with a distinct goal in mind. She wanted to raise children who valued a relationship with Christ more than earthly treasure. From their infancy, she taught them to love God and treasure His Word. As they grew, she stressed to them the extreme importance of not living for this world. While she instructed them in good etiquette, manners, and proper behavior, she also kept before them the true goal of life—to follow the Lord's leading and trust His wisdom for the future. Sherry and her husband James modeled the kind of life they taught. As good stewards of their financial resources, they were willing to drive older cars that often needed repairs and postpone a bigger house so they could afford to send their children to a Christian school where they could gain a godly worldview. Sherry took a job to pay the monthly tuition. She and her husband didn't take nice vacations or dine in restaurants very often or have extra funds for hobbies. They invested everything they could into the training of their children—both their time and money. There were difficult times, but each of their three children graduated from a Christian college and today, all are involved in Christian ministry. And God has blessed James and Sherry with some of the benefits they didn't have in earlier years. But if they'd never been able to have a nice home or car, they wouldn't regret a single sacrifice they made. They believed it was more important to store up treasure "on the other side" through carefully guiding the hearts and minds of their children. And that's why today, Sherry's children "rise up" in praise of a mother who taught them to see beyond the present to the eternal riches no one can take away.

Our culture is characterized by the inordinate desire for more. The fast pace of technological advances insures that what we crave today will be obsolete tomorrow. The competition between marketers to gain the public's loyalty and dollars guarantees that there will always be some new toy, gadget, or automobile calling to us from the shop window. Like the glossy fruit dangling in front of

Eve, the luscious offerings of our affluent society lay before us. If we would escape the trap of greed and teach our children to do the same, we must focus on gaining a heart that is content—a happy heart.

The pathway to a happy heart is discipline and surrender to the God who has ordered the framework of our lives and discipline in the daily management of it. In my own journey through motherhood, I have discovered that I cannot teach my children what I have not accepted myself. So, as we move toward greater contentment ourselves, we can patiently and consistently teach them as well. We can put it into practice by helping them to:

1. Be satisfied with limited options; too many choices could make a child hard to please.

2. Be aware of others' lack; this will counteract the "life's not fair to me" attitude.

3. Be careful in words; cautiously use the word *deserve*; entitlement is the plague of our culture.

4. Be watchful of boasting; one blogging mother says you should not let your children talk about the things they get—for Christmas or birthdays especially, which keeps the spotlight on accumulating things.

5. Be wary of marketing messages; try to limit their exposure to advertising.

6. Be focused on blessings; there will always be something you don't have; accept that as being normal.

7. Be delighted; life abounds with simple pleasures for those who look for them.

Responding through Prayer

Dear Father, You've given me children to nurture for You. They belong to You; I am the steward, the caretaker of Your precious treasure. Give me wisdom to teach them principles about contentment and discernment that will guide them even when they are on their own someday. May they mature into adults who have the right perspective of wealth and ambition. I ask You to protect them from Satan's deception. Help me model for them an attitude of thankfulness for the blessings our family enjoys. In Christ's name. Amen.

My Next Step

To help my children learn to discern what is really valuable in life, I will:

- Be aware of my spending habits and the message that relays to them.
- Teach them at least two Scripture verses that deal with appropriate priorities.
-
-

Keep It in Mind

Imagine your children twenty-five years from now. What guiding principles do you want to see in their lives in the areas of perspective and contentment? Begin today to teach them about the true value in life so you can leave them the legacy of a happy heart. "Her children arise and call her blessed" (Prov. 31:28).

7

The Success Syndrome

Matthew 25:14–30

*So if you have not been trustworthy in handling worldly
wealth, who will trust you with true riches?*

—Luke 16:11

Discovery

True success is measured by faithfulness and contentment, not by
financial assets.

For Openers

Facebook has changed the way we interact with friends and
family. It is the twenty-first-century front porch, the place to
gather and share. Frankly, I am a fan of the many benefits of this
social network. I have been able to reconnect with high school
friends, see photos of family members in other states, and be
aware of urgent prayer needs affecting those I know. I have also

been able to stay in touch with acquaintances needing words of encouragement and affirmation. It has blessed me in many ways.

But on this earth, few things come without some negatives. There are those who disparage Facebook, and some of their points are valid (though it hasn't yet caused me to delete my profile). Facebook allows us to put our best foot forward, so to speak. We can un-tag unflattering photos, carefully word our statuses, and describe our personal information in complimentary ways. We can concentrate on projecting the best image possible, and most of us do.

The Facebook syndrome pushes us to look for some new achievement or acquisition about which to post. Each of us wants to share something that will be lauded by our friends. We want to be held in high regard; it's nice to receive affirmation. It's fun to have a new success to type into the status box.

Getting to Know Her

Once, there were three employees who worked for an exclusive clothing manufacturer—Carrie, Jo, and Shirley. Seeing promise in these women, the owner wanted to determine if they were worthy of greater advancement in the corporation. She decided to test them.

One day, she called all three into her office and put a file into each of their hands. In the file, she explained, were the names of clients with whom the firm would like to increase business. While she took an extended leave of absence, she was asking them to develop these opportunities for the benefit of the company. She did not tell them that the three files were not the same; for it was at her discretion that she distributed the list of clients to each, knowing whose personality and skills were best for the ones they were to contact.

Her trip took longer than she originally anticipated, but after six months, she returned. She could hardly wait to meet with her protégés to see what they had accomplished. Carrie gave her report first, offering the paperwork that showed she had doubled the amount of investment from the clients. Jo, also, had done remarkably well, again doubling the size of her own portfolio. The owner was noticing that Shirley seemed a little anxious, shifting her weight and clearing her throat. And when she gave her report, the owner understood why. She hadn't done anything! Not only had she not gained any business for the firm, she hadn't even tried! The owner could hardly believe her ears as Shirley confessed she'd been so frightened of making the clients mad that she had carefully tucked the file into a drawer for safekeeping. At least the clients listed on it were still customers.

The owner was livid. Shirley had let her fears determine her actions. She terminated Shirley's employment and handed her file to Carrie. She knew she could be trusted to fulfill her responsibility.

The Word Speaks

You've probably guessed by now that the vignette above is a retelling of Jesus' parable in **Matthew 25:14-30**—usually called the parable of the talents. Take a few minutes to read the story in the Bible.

It's easy to see that the servant with the one talent (Shirley) failed, while the other two clearly achieved commendation. Do you know the reason for Shirley's failure? She used the wrong measure for success. She represents the idea that success is measured by a certain level of prosperity and power. Fearing her skills could not match the demand, she chose simply not to try at all.

She didn't see that she was expected only to be diligent in completing her assignment. She was not to get caught up in worrying about the outcome. She was not to compare her skills with those of Carrie or Jo. She was to accept the task she had been given and perform it faithfully. If she had done that, she also would have received a promotion, bonus, and the personal praise of the owner.

Where We Come In

Maybe you don't work for a high-end corporation, but you're acquainted with the success syndrome. Maybe it would more accurately be called the success cycle, because once it begins, it's difficult to stop. A little taste of prestige and glamour is never enough. The desire for more is forever influencing the decisions and lifestyle of those who buy into its system.

There is no contentment in the success cycle, because success has come to mean an endless quest for what is bigger and better. And some parts of the globe feel this struggle more keenly than others.

Discontent is a malady of civilized nations. Oddly enough, the people who have the most stuff are the least content. Those in Third World countries rarely struggle with it; they are too focused on survival.

In the 1940s, a psychologist named Abraham Maslow researched the topic of human motivation and created a model he called the hierarchy of needs. In this pyramid-shaped diagram, he charts what could be called the layers of life. The foundational layer has to do with the basic necessities of survival—water, food, and shelter. Once those needs are met, humans become concerned with the next level, safety, then on to love and belonging. The order of motivation is always from the bottom level up. If the lower tiers of need are suddenly washed away, concern for the top tiers will be replaced once again by the basic survival instinct. This means that only those who have the luxury of attaining the top level will have to battle discontent. Prosperity begets other struggles.

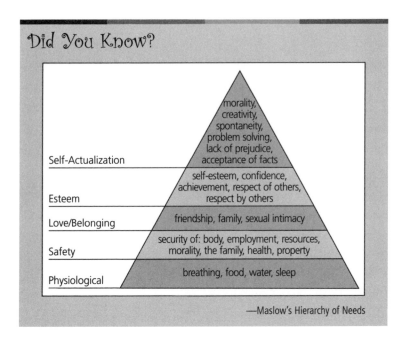

Did You Know?

Self-Actualization	morality, creativity, spontaneity, problem solving, lack of prejudice, acceptance of facts
Esteem	self-esteem, confidence, achievement, respect of others, respect by others
Love/Belonging	friendship, family, sexual intimacy
Safety	security of: body, employment, resources, morality, the family, health, property
Physiological	breathing, food, water, sleep

—Maslow's Hierarchy of Needs

This is important in our understanding of contentment. Our ancestors probably didn't worry about contentment; they were focused on putting bread on the table and working the land. As America has prospered, her citizens have become more and more obsessed with the pursuit of happiness to their own detriment. Our founders never meant for our freedoms to become our addictions. When they do, we find ourselves slaves to the acquisition of prosperity.

In the last few decades, there has been a popular notion that God financially prospers those who love Him. There are some who interpret scriptural promises of blessing to mean financial, material, and physical benefits. And even those believers who don't espouse the so-called prosperity gospel may lean toward an indulgent interpretation of the abundant life promised by Jesus in John 10:10.

During a difficult financial time in our family, I was listening to Christian radio in my car. Featured on a lunch-hour talk show was a panel of women discussing how God delights in giving us the things we desire. One woman told how she really wanted to go to Europe and God provided the tickets just to show her He loved her. Another panelist shared that she had always wanted a grand piano (she didn't play the piano, but she thought they were pretty). And, she reported, God had simply given her a piano to put in her home.

While I firmly believe that God delights in giving us good things, I strongly disagree with the conclusion of these women. God doesn't show His love by giving us toys; He proved His love beyond any doubt on a cross long ago. He may choose to bless us or not, but He is good all the time.

In blessed America, we've come to think that abundant life means God is letting us live the good life. But that isn't what Jesus had in mind. You see, the abundant life is a promise to every believer, even those in Third World countries. If prosperity is part of the mix, Christians on the other side of the world are being gypped.

Look at Luke 12:15: "For a man's life does not consist in and is not derived from possessing overflowing abundance or that which is over and above his needs" (AMP).

What Others Say

It is a constant battle to resist the temptation to have more luxuries, to acquire more stuff, and to live more comfortably. It requires strong and steady resolve to live out the gospel in the middle of an American dream that identifies success as moving up the ladder, getting the bigger house, purchasing the nicer car, buying the better clothes, eating the finer food, and acquiring more things.

—David Platt

Of course, remembering our discussion in the first chapter, there is nothing innately wrong with nice things, and it isn't evil for a woman to enjoy shopping. But it wouldn't hurt us to adjust our perspective a little in this area. Maybe, instead of hitting the shops to spend money we don't have, we can go shopping simply to enjoy the colors, textures, and artistic drape and fold and cut of fabric. Maybe, we can drink in the beauty of lovely table settings at the home decorating store without needing to own them. Maybe we can give ourselves some boundaries and within them, find freedom to buy what we need when we need it and feel free from the pressure the other times.

How It Works Today

Melodie had a wonderful life with her pastor-husband, Marc, and their three sons. She was fulfilled and happy in her role as wife, mom, and ministry partner. When God called their family to mission work in the interior of Mexico, Melodie struggled to accept this dramatic change in her life. Moving away from their congregation and families was painful. With her husband in language school in Texas, Melodie found herself often feeling isolated, even in the grocery store where she was the only English-speaking person. She began to learn Spanish and was determined to thrive in her new setting. During their time in Mexico, Melodie's family faced some serious health issues. In these dark times, Melodie learned new levels of trust. She realized anew that following Christ doesn't guarantee the absence of troubles, but promises the presence of the Comforter. She learned about real value and discovered that contentment is something entirely different than the notion of middle-class Americans. The sincere believers in Mexico had little in earthly possessions but possessed genuine spiritual wealth. They weren't caught up in the success syndrome that entangles so many in more affluent cultures. In an interview shortly after they returned to the States, Melodie said she hoped she could keep the perspective she gained in Mexico. Living the American dream isn't at the top of her list; having an authentically Christian life is. Embracing Jesus' love for people instead of possessions makes a life truly successful. And that's her goal wherever God calls her to live.

No matter what I buy today, there will be something else to tempt me tomorrow. You can never stay ahead of the stuff game. The appetite for another pretty thing will be just as strong next week as it is today. Contentment is finding the courage to say, "I have enough for now," and finding that there is freedom indeed in the realization.

Maybe we should text this verse to ourselves and look at it often while we're on a shopping spree: "So if we have enough food and clothing, let us be content" (1 Tim. 6:8 NLT).

> ### What Others Say
>
> It is good for a man's soul to know what he can do without.
>
> —Aristotle

In times past, God prospered those who served Him because He "was forming a nation for himself that would be a demonstration of his greatness to all other nations."[1] Today, He doesn't prosper us so we can build magnificent temples or display to others His greatness. He blesses some with financial wealth so that they can share with others who need it. Those who are not wealthy are not loved less; they merely have a different place to fill in the kingdom. And He never intends our prosperity to finance our personal indulgences.

Read James 4:3. God doesn't answer us with dollars we can squander on ourselves. He distributes wealth for His glory and the blessing of others who are less fortunate.

As believers, we need to step back and assess the model of success we have embraced. If we think like the culture, we will be frustrated because it believes that possessions and power determine happiness. If we have accepted the biblical model of stewardship, we can be content knowing that we are only caretakers of the life, possessions, and family God has given us. What we have really belongs to Him; we can be free from the pressure of the success syndrome.

The one who is a caretaker looks out for the interests of her Master; she is not preoccupied with increasing her own wealth, but in building up His assets. She doesn't harbor an inflated opinion of herself or her position. She wants to be successful as a servant, in doing everything diligently and for His glory. The commendation she craves is the words, "Well done, good and faithful servant."

Responding through Prayer

Heavenly Father, give me spiritual wisdom to see more clearly that everything I am and own is a sacred trust from You. Guard my heart from being caught up in the success syndrome of the culture which is built on greed for possessions and power. Let me see my daily routines as the highest service for You and enable me to complete my tasks with diligence and faithfulness so that someday I can hear you say, "Well done." In Jesus' name. Amen.

My Next Step

To combat the effects of the success syndrome, this week, I will:

■

■

Keep It in Mind

Faithful stewardship is success. When we joyfully and faithfully manage what He has given us, not only will we be content, but we can also be assured of His commendation. "Whoever can be trusted with very little can also be trusted with much" (Luke 16:10).

8

Now or Later

Genesis 16

*For where your treasure is,
there your heart will be also.*

—Matthew 6:21

Discovery

To experience real contentment, I must reject the "get it now" culture and embrace the concept of delayed gratification as it pertains to both my earthly life and eternity.

For Openers

For all its valuable lessons in management and financial responsibility, Monopoly is somewhat a game of greed. To do well at the game, you should possess Scrooge-like tendencies. I was never good at it because inevitably I would cave in, accepting half the rent payment for the properties I owned, for example.

This is not to say that I have no greedy tendencies, rather, it affirms that I would not make a good office manager!

Those who understand the game of Monopoly know that the object of the game is acquiring property, which means, initially, you have to spend quite a bit. In order to own Park Place and put a few houses on it, you have to shell out the bucks. But a few turns later, you're collecting big-time rent from all the other suckers on the board. In a classic game Americans have enjoyed for decades, Parker Brothers clearly illustrated the concept of delayed gratification—things of real value are worth the wait.

Getting to Know Her

Impatience is the curse of those who would learn contentment. **Genesis 16** tells the story of the consequences of impatience. Take time to read this chapter now. The woman's name was Sarah. God had promised her husband, Abraham, that he would have more descendants than he could count. But she was old and barren. She was tired of waiting. She told her husband to take a second wife— her maid, in fact. According to the custom of the time, her personal slave was her property, and anything that belonged to the slave belonged to the mistress. So if Hagar were to conceive, the child would legally belong to Sarah.[1]

Abraham did as Sarah asked— maybe to keep peace, maybe because he longed for the promised

> **Bible Background**
>
> Hagar was Egyptian, likely a slave girl acquired from the Pharaoh who took Sarah for his harem and gave Abraham gifts in exchange for his "sister." (You can read the story in Gen. 12:14–20.) Her name was Hebrew and meant a "stranger or sojourner."

child as much as she, but also maybe because of his love for Sarah. He knew how much she wanted a child, and he was willing to do whatever he could, even if it was awkward or unsavory to him, to give her the chance to have one. After all, she was past childbearing years. And what she asked was not out of the ordinary at that time.

Hagar conceived and gave birth to a son whom God named Ishmael. But he was not to be Abraham's heir of promise. It was ten years later that God fulfilled His covenant with a son from Sarah's womb. But her impatience had complicated things. The desire for gratification on her timetable caused pain to her family, to Hagar and Ishmael, and many others. And so we often will find it in our lives.

The Word Speaks

Read 1 Timothy 6:6–10. The apostle Paul wrote to young Timothy about an important theme—money and prosperity. He focused on the end of life. He stated a fact that we all know so well—we cannot take anything with us when we die. Verse 10 has often been misquoted. What does the Bible actually call the root of all kinds of evil?

Greed is an attitude of impatience in regards to what one prizes highly. When people are consumed with the desire to have their chief joy, they will stoop to any level to acquire it—lying, cheating, killing, and more. If you want to unleash the potential for the whole gamut of sinfulness in your life, give yourself over to greed.

Now read Matthew 6:19–33. In the Sermon on the Mount, Jesus told His listeners to decide what they valued and their investments would reflect it. Whoever possesses our devotion owns the bank account. Dr. Joseph Stowell says, "Many of us are concerned that if we commit ourselves as fully devoted followers, Christ will threaten the treasury. He probably will. . . . We can't have it both ways. We either let Him be the master of our money, or our money will master us."[2]

Money deceives many people into false worship; it even seems to offer the same benefits as Christ. In their book *Living in Light of Eternity*, Stacy and Paul Rinehart say, "Money is a rival god. . . . Having a seductive power all its own, money is capable of inspiring devotion, of giving us a false sense of security, freedom, and omnipotence."[3]

We live in a credit-card happy, debt-soaked society. Our national debt is more than we can ever repay, and many of the households in the nation are on the doorstep of bankruptcy. It's really amazing how credit card companies stalk potential clients. Our mailboxes are regularly graced with a letter or two promising pre-approved credit and low interest rates. Do you know what they are actually saying? "Don't wait; indulge now."

Does this mean credit cards are evil? Well, if you can't control them, they might be. But when used appropriately, of course not! The problem is that our culture has increasingly craved indulgence in ways we cannot afford. So we enjoy them anyway before we have even paid for them. We are a culture of immediate gratification.

Jesus told us to focus on the eternal, the "not now." Instead of worrying about clothing and food, zero in on the real needs of life: a right relationship with God and the glory of His kingdom. Then He will take care of our needs and we will be content. We will be free to live as He intends when we let Him be in charge.

Where We Come In

To practice delayed gratification requires that we live with our gaze fixed on eternity. To be free from obsession of material things and the greed for more and more, we must embrace Jesus' words and value what is truly important—eternal treasure. Heaven is the place where we will experience final and complete fulfillment. Our everyday lives reveal where we're investing.

What Others Say

All of life can be divided into two simple categories: the perishable and the imperishable. . . . God wants us to turn our attention to what is lasting, what has permanent value because it is a reflection of His own nature.

—Stacy and Paul Rinehart

Turn to Luke 12:16–21. From an eternal perspective, it is foolish to make this earth the primary source of investment. This wealthy man made plans to store up goods for his retirement and then settled down to enjoy temporal pleasures. He gave himself over to an indulgent way of life. It was all about this life. He neglected to consider that death would separate him from his earthly savings. He had made no preparation for eternity. "This is how it will be with anyone stores up things for himself but is not rich toward God" (v. 21).

In what ways have you been tempted to focus on today and ignore eternity?

Everything temporal will be left here someday. "Like a mother calling her children while they are at play, death will soon gather us from our sand piles to depart."[4] And then, we will own only what we have deposited in heaven's account.

Did You Know?

The word translated "barns" in Luke 12:18 is from the Greek *apotithêmi*, meaning to lay by, to treasure. It bears the sense of a granary or storehouse. Perhaps Jesus had this in mind when He told those listening to store treasure in heaven where moths and vermin can't destroy it (Matt. 6:20).

Jesus asked this question, "What good is it for a man to gain the whole world, yet forfeit his soul?" (Mark 8:36). We are souls, whose bodies are only expressions of the persons who live in them. Losing the soul is not like misplacing it somewhere, but rather it is disregarding its intrinsic value and thereby condemning it to an uncertain eternity. Those who understand the soul's worth invariably store assets in that other world for which it is bound. As the apostle Paul said in Philippians 1:21, "For to me, to live is Christ and to die is gain."

Now read Ecclesiastes 2:1–11. This is the record of a foolish experiment in the life of one of the wisest men who ever lived. He decided to see if there was happiness to be found in indulging his every whim. And he had the resources to do it. The verses record that he denied himself nothing he wanted, but there was no lasting pleasure in it. Like grasping at a breeze, it eluded him. Such is the conclusion of all who indulge in immediate earthly gratification—it does not satisfy.

Take a few minutes to discuss some barriers to overindulgence that you can erect for your own spiritual welfare.

How It Works Today

Heather likes fine things. Her mother instilled in her both an appreciation for well-crafted antiques and a preference for refinement in daily living. Their dining room table never lacked a floral centerpiece, even if it came from the field beside the house, and the family always used china and crystal on Sundays. Now serving Christ in foreign missions with her husband and five children, Heather has had to adapt in many kinds of circumstances. Their first residence in a strange land was in the home of parishioners where all they could call home was a bedroom of their own. And when they finally had a home of their own, there were some things she still had to be flexible about. But Heather enjoys her role as homemaker, keeping her simple home neat and lovely and cooking homemade meals for her family. She knows that beautiful antiques are only temporary treasures; they are susceptible to deterioration. But heaven is her real home, where nothing will decay and everything lasts forever. So she and her husband Phillip are using their energies to point others toward that better country because they know that the best is yet to come.

Like those of faith before us, we know that we are "foreigners and nomads here on earth" (Heb. 11:13 NLT). Instead of fixing our gaze on this temporary home, we are looking toward a "better country—a heavenly one," where God has prepared a city for us (Heb. 11:16).

Read again Matthew 6:20–21. Heaven is the storehouse of the wise. Its treasure never corrodes or is stolen. And its pleasures are

What Others Say

Our Father refreshes us on the journey with some pleasant inns, but will not encourage us to mistake them for home.

—C. S. Lewis

eternal. "In Your presence is fullness of joy; at Your right hand are pleasures forevermore" (Ps. 16:11 NKJV).

Responding through Prayer

Lord, thank you for the earthly blessings I have. Help me to view them as gifts from You. Where I have gained them by means other than Your will, forgive me and make me wiser so that I will not reach for things beyond what You ordain for me. Let me have the proper perspective of temporal assets. Teach me to value eternal treasures so highly that I will be eager to invest in Your kingdom. I don't want to fall prey to the seduction of immediate gratification. I ask that You would guard my mind and direct my desires to goals that honor You, for yours is the kingdom, and the power, and the glory forever. In Christ's name. Amen.

My Next Step

Realizing that the Bible calls me to value heavenly riches, this week, I will invest in eternity by:

- Selecting a credible kingdom-building project to which I can financially contribute as God enables me.
- Donating some time to a worthy ministry—women's crisis centers, homeless shelters, urban youth outreach, etc.
-
-

Keep It in Mind

In a culture characterized by a "get it now" attitude, we must fix our eyes on the wealth of eternity and make choices that reflect this priority. To be truly free from the culture of excess, we must look beyond what makes us happy today to what will bring everlasting joy. "We consider and look not to the things that are seen but to the things that are unseen; for the things that are visible are temporal (brief and fleeting), but the things that are invisible are deathless and everlasting" (2 Cor. 4:18 AMP).

Notes

Chapter 2

1. Kelly Minter, *No Other Gods: Confronting our Modern Day Idols* (Colorado Springs: David C. Cook, 2008), 13.
2. Charles Dickens, *A Christmas Carol* (New York: Penguin, 2008), 2.

Chapter 3

1. Alison E. Field, et al., "Exposure to the Mass Media and Weight Concerns Among Girls," *Official Journal of the American Academy of Pediatrics* 103, no. 3 (March 1, 1999), e36, http://pediatrics.aap publications.org/content/103/3/e36.full.
2. Ibid.

Chapter 4

1. The Statler Brothers, "The Class of '57," accessed December 8, 2011, http://www.metrolyrics.com/class-of-57-lyrics-the-statler-brothers.html.
2. Elisabeth Elliot, *Be Still My Soul* (Grand Rapids, Mich.: Revell, 2003), 35.

3. John Piper, *Desiring God: Meditations of a Christian Hedonist* (Colorado Springs: Multnomah Books, 2003), 166.

4. Amy Carmichael, *Toward Jerusalem* (CLC Ministries, 1988).

Chapter 7

1. David Platt, *Radical: Taking Back Your Faith from the American Dream* (Colorado Springs: Multnomah, 2010), 116.

Chapter 8

1. Adam Clarke, *The Holy Bible with Commentary and Critical Notes* (Baltimore, Md.: John Harrod, 1834), 123.

2. Joseph M. Stowell, *Following Christ: Experiencing Life the Way It Was Meant to Be* (Grand Rapids, Mich.: Zondervan, 1996), 144.

3. Stacy and Paula Rinehart, *Living in Light of Eternity: How to Base Your Life on What Really Matters* (Colorado Springs: NavPress, 1986), 98.

4. Ibid., 84.